Little Wild

LITTLE

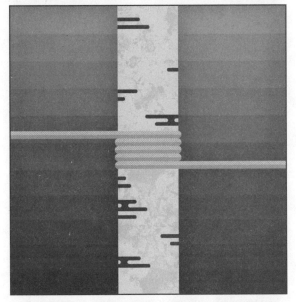

WILD

CURTIS LEBLANC

NIGHTWOOD EDITIONS

2018

Nightwood Editions
P.O. Box 1779
Gibsons, BC VON 1V0
Canada
www.nightwoodeditions.com

EDITOR: Carleton Wilson
COVER DESIGN: Erik Grice
TYPESETTING: Carleton Wilson

Canada

Nightwood Editions acknowledges financial support from
the Government of Canada and the Canada Council for the Arts,
and from the Province of British Columbia through
the British Columbia Arts Council and the Book Publisher's Tax Credit.

This book has been produced on 100% post-consumer recycled,
ancient-forest-free paper, processed chlorine-free
and printed with vegetable-based dyes.

Printed and bound in Canada.

CIP data available from Library and Archives Canada.

ISBN 978-0-88971-337-6

For my parents,
Ann & Marcel

Contents

I

Good for Nothing

I had to fall off a ladder to the stars

and break my right forearm and flunk calculus
so as predicted at my initial birth
I'd be good for nothing but to tell you this.

—Philip Levine

Narrowing

I used to bathe in shallow water
until it lost all warmth, ignore toy trolls
and colour-changing plastic dolls
to pick caulking from the corners
where off-white tiles met porcelain tub.
I would pull at the gummy seams,
fingers sponged and wrinkled, until
my father came to dry me off.
His shoulders hunched, peppery curls
combed always to the left, he'd beat his chest
and howl like an ape, smack the walls
with his hands and bounce on the balls
of his feet, and I'd laugh and laugh
and hold my own arms out for him
to lift me, wrap me in an even heat.

Now here we are, damp
from our separate showers,
and ready for sleep, or nearly.
He asks me again, *Who have you
hurt today?* Refuses to see
that the answer is *No one*,
that his eyes are mine and
his shoulders have narrowed.
Same ten-dollar strip mall haircut,
little wild left in either of us.

Steel-Cut Oats

One small pot of steel-cut oats
on the stove, glutenous, ladled
into my bowl despite my contempt.
Mom said they would be as good
as the instant variety. Better even.
But too little brown sugar, absence
of additives—what they lacked in flavour,
they made up for in mouth feel. I gagged
with each spoonful, seated at the island
in the kitchen where every day I sat eating
one thing or another. But not this.
Do what I say, she said. Never
in her life had she seen a child
so ungrateful, me on the kitchen stool,
made to scoop the pale gruel
through the crack of my lips
until nothing was left in the blue
plastic bowl. I had never been held
to anything like she had been held to
that afternoon behind the cashier's counter
at the bank in Londonderry Mall, a sawed-off
shotgun pressed to her chest, told to fill
a duffle bag with petty cash.
Do what they say, was protocol
back then. Get help
after the threat has left.

Blood in a Place I Could Not Yet Understand

It was harder to say no back then,
when Paul threatened to sue me
after I told him I wouldn't play
GI Joe beneath the weevil-chewed spruce
on the island of my cul-de-sac where he
always came to visit his aunt. I liked him fine.
He told stories as tall as that spruce, sometimes
taller. But when he tracked dog shit all through
my house, even on the tie-dye beanbag
chair in my basement, that meant we
were finished. That was how I saw it then.
But I couldn't see why Paul wore that one rip-off
Mighty Ducks jersey even in the off-season,
lived for entire weeks with his uncle and aunt
when his adoptive mother was seven blocks
away, his parents by blood in a place
I could not yet understand. It wasn't until
high school that I saw the things they wrote
about him in the *St. Albert Gazette*—thirty round
white pills of OxyContin, stormwater
and spring thaw breaking around his body spread
like discarded clothing in the concrete basin
at the bottom of the ravine behind my cul-de-sac.

A Letter from Scandinavia

Where is he when his son's dog hangs?
Not close enough to hear the scratches
echo from the tunnel slide, see the leash
tied up at the top of the jungle gym,
the dog at the other end, pawing
smooth hard plastic. Two cops bag it
like dirty laundry, heave it into the cruiser.
The father holds a felt blanket over
his son, smooths the creases down his back,
guides his shoulders with firm hands,
lifts his chin with one finger to the men
in uniform. The boy describes the ones
who did it and it's a manhunt. Neighbours
accuse each other's children. Police
interrogations in the schools. Sympathizers
go in bunches with flowers for his family,
bake them apple rhubarb pies, whisper
in convenience stores and parking lots
about the boy who had to watch
his poor dog die.

They receive, the father
estimates, one hundred calls and messages.
Steady mail, even a letter from Scandinavia
from a couple that breeds Finnish dogs,
reindeer herders. *Lapphunds*, they call them.
His family can have one if they'd like.
The story is out and the world has chosen
to stand by. The father wants nothing more
to do with it. But still he keeps that letter close,
thumbs the corners of it, holds it like a prize.

He considers writing the Scandinavians
but hasn't settled on what to type.
He wants to tell them, *We're coming,*
we're just about to board the plane,
and by the time that you receive this
we will have come and gone already.
He spends weeks thinking of how to put it
in exactly the right words, how grateful
he was to receive their letter, how
he has read it over a dozen times. He wants
to tell them how he folds it into quarters,
always along the same creases,
through words like *acreage*, *obedient*,
suffering, *sincerely*.

                    Later, his son admits it
was an accident. Tied the leash himself
and then went down the slide. The dog,
a good one, had gone to follow.
The ones who believed the boy want
to see him punished, put to shame.
But the father thinks that he can feel it,
what his son must have felt right then,
watching his best friend put paw over paw,
each step slipping like the last. He knows,
at the very least, that it's a lesson
best learned young: to tell a lie and give
it up, before you have to shoulder it
for what will be, with any luck, a long life.

An Outdoor Education

Lengths of rope meant for lean-tos,
for securing the corners of a tarp to tree trunks,
were used instead to hog-tie my beanpole body
to a dried-out birch during outdoor education class.
Those other kids—friends of mine, I'd say still—started
with my shins and wound the whiskered yellow nylon cord
around and around until I couldn't shift, arms cinched to my side,
papery white bark curling up the ass of my jeans. They doused
my thighs in lighter fluid then traced the dark stain
with the lick of a Zippo flame until I became the first branch
catching on a pyre. But the butane burned
clean through to cotton threads that did not catch.
I was left with nothing but a heat rash.
You have been the only thing to ever change me.

Sunbathers

Every day back then we did a few good things. Stayed put, sunbathed
on the front of the Honda outside Beaver Lumber, waited for our fathers
to return with bundles of pinewood one-by-fours—clearance aisle dry
material for our neighbourhood tree fort. Years later, we sunbathers

waded through the front doors of Totem Hardware, stole, as adolescents
do, valves in bags of free popcorn for a beer bong we hit in those dry-
rotted tree forts. We were spotted in the clearing by the neighbours
who then told our fathers. They still thought we were better

than teens sucking beer through popcorn-greased ball valves and
vinyl tubing. Then they discovered the stash of papers we'd promised
to deliver. Who told our fathers we could have been better? To think
it was the fort they helped us build that we'd been hiding them beneath.

Eventually, after they discovered those papers, they delivered on
their promise, returned the pinewood planks to a bundle and burned
them. For our fathers, it helped to hide all that beneath—to build
oneself, *d'être fort*—and every day stay a doer of a few good things.

Categorical Imperative

*Act in such a way that you treat humanity, whether in your own
person or in the person of any other, never merely as a means to an
end, but always at the same time as an end.*

—Immanuel Kant

I find the cat deflated on the washing room floor
beneath dark damp denims and blouses wrinkled
in the armpits and at the cuffs. My mother scoops
it with a towel, into the carrier cage. In two days
I'll turn twelve years old and go on
loving this cat that goes on living

in my head, attached to a heart rate monitor
and a tiny IV at the vet clinic. The truth is my parents
find it dead in the backseat before it ever makes it
to medical attention. There is no salvation to be had,
save for the twelfth birthday party, unfurled
noisemakers, a surprise spared on my behalf.

One day after, my parents confess and I thank them
for their small deception—one that I can never manage
since the serotonin flush in the synapses of my brain
made a categorical imperative out of everything
I do or say. Can't goodwill be enough to relieve me?

If I am right then wrong is just an illness.

Imperatives

At Turtle Lake, we learned to water-ski
on a wooden door tethered to
your family's speedboat. We'd scan
the surface for the long shadow
of the monster, that old myth, slipping
through algae blooms and split pines.
A sturgeon, your mother said. You and I
were boys with favourite porn stars,
preferred ways to build a fire. We left out
the back door, a blowtorch taped to the knob
of a hockey stick, burned a wasp nest
on your mother's orders. You couldn't stand it
when she told us to sleep, pointed her finger,
killing the light as we leafed through comics
in the framed shade of antique bunk beds.

Not long ago, she summoned your body
back from Mexico. Your older brothers
carried it—to and from the front of the church,
in and out the back of the hearse—to where
she asked you to rest for the last time.

Oldman River Dam

My father never learned to swim. His sisters,
all eight of them, keep the reason close

to their chests at annual Rainmaker Rodeo hot-dog
roasts and holiday dinners. He and my mother

once rode a river cruise down the Danube,
cabined next door to the engine room. The hum

was one of dry land, pole-mounted transformers
and distant traffic. In this, he found his comfort.

When I was ten, we drove with my brother
and sister to Drumheller, played dinosaur soup

inside a plastic cast-iron pot. A stegosaurus statue
stirred away overtop, a photographic opportunity

featuring us as raw ingredients. On the way
home, we stopped at the Oldman River Dam,

where in the visitor centre, there's a plaque
with my father's name on it. At the walkway's

lookout, mist beading on the back of his neck,
he pointed out the ways he'd had a say

in holding the river back. He was schooled as a man
of retention ponds and culverts, to remove

all mystery from the downward run of water.
On an Easter when one sister drank enough

of Pépère's punch, she told him, *You know,*
still waters are the worst to drown in.

Folded Up Like a Coward on the Night of the Dance

Once I won an award for an essay
on the importance of keeping sober.
It was written in the rough scrawl
of an eleven-year-old—a miracle
the cop could read it after he collected
all the loose-leaf from class. I got sick then,
muffled with an oxygen mask
in Emergency, and couldn't read my paper
at Drug Abuse Resistance Education grad.
Robert McClure read his paper instead
and he cried on stage for my inflamed lungs,
his fire-orange hair just long enough
at the bangs to become damp with the salt water
pinched from his pink-rimmed eyelids.

Two years later I watched my friends soak
every weekend with malt liquor. In twos
and threes they sought the shade
of man-made hills, the partial cover
of a sudden stand of poplars, pulled smoke
like blue cloth from the cores of gala apples.
They poured themselves over bannisters, filled
the idle fountains of West Edmonton Mall.
I leaned against the school bleachers, folded up
like a coward on the night of the dance,
resisted music in the unlit gym, inhaled
distilled sweat, hardwood turpentine stench.
All in secret interest.

I was fifteen when that first cough
of Kokanee came in Trace Kramer's hot tub.
That taught me I needed to acquire a taste,
so I took to light beer every night for a week
in bed, borrowed from the fridge
in our unfinished basement. It was a measured
prelude to water-bottle shit mix, coconut rum,
whichever twelve-pack was the cheapest.
Every pint glass pulled from the freezer since,
filled and emptied and filled again.
Those sober thoughts I couldn't stand to miss—
I do my best now to keep them quiet.

Charnel House

I make my bed and think of Abby,
her house haunted by a ghost who,
through the slow erratic grating
of plastic on a Ouija board,
called himself Fez.
We were young then, given to
the dark magic in our fingertips,
convinced by the butcher's knife
that balanced on the bannister.
We lit tea lights, coaxed spirits
into speech with a cardboard alphabet,
asking, "Why is this a haunted place?"
The reply was a phrase
we later found out meant
a house in which the dead are kept
among some other things:
televisions that turned themselves
off and on to static, cold breath
from basement walls,
cupboards that slammed
in smaller hours, unapologetic.
There was a bed, still made,
where her mother no longer slept.
Her father's bed was the couch back then.
Still is, for all I know.

Sonnet for the Driveways of Our Childish Years

All the tennis balls that our Gretzky curves
couldn't guide past the taut rubber screen
of a Shooter Tutor cratered the garage door.
Personal moons for the parties we missed,
where some young men made the porch-like climb
to violence. When I was sixteen, I knew a kid
who got his face stomped on the curb, lost his two
front teeth on the concrete foot of his own front lawn.
We heard stories like that every day, dribbled down
the driveways of this northernmost America.
Shaq's hand burned into our basketballs, dishing
high-fives to the pavement, eclipsing our palms.
Forced outdoors by our fathers and mothers,
we learned to forget each other and be alone.

Sociables

after Troy Snaterse

I could have sworn I saw you, Mitch,
head shaved for the summer's big encore,
September Long, riding the gummy wheels
of your pool board down Fair Oaks Drive
to Marina's house. Relish on your tank top,
mustard dusting the corners of your mouth.
Arms tanned the colour of iced tea and a burn
on your hand from when you were given to dreams
with the roach in your mouth. You were a boy
who wanted nothing more than to play Red Hot
Chili Peppers on the bass guitar. We never let you,
stuck on the tired lines of "Boxcar" and "Brown Eyed Girl."
And on your second shift when the forklift tipped
on a hairpin turn, you were riding the side like a boy
might do. Mitch, you died as you lived: rolling
a load on four wheels with no knowledge
of the purpose. You, a kid crushed breathless
in the warehouse of Home Hardware, working
to afford Chucks and spliffs and Olde English 800.
Where we're from is like any place else.
You've got to work to go to Peach Fest, smoke Captains,
play Sociables. Was it enough? All the times we sat
around a coffee table drawing up the rules—boys drink,
girls drink, beer fetcher, box head—and all of us
promising we wouldn't break the circle.

Gravel Pit

Always more bottles than able mouths
nights out on the Hagan family farm.
Deer shit in quad trail ruts.

Property billboards
advertised casino breakfasts
off the Whitecourt exit nearby.

I drove drunk to the gravel pit,
one Hagan holding on to the hood
of his token Ford truck,

yelling, *Faster!*
through the windshield.
Faster, you little fuck!

We were going for a swim,
sweating and naked, all of us
holding the deadweight of the others up.

We offered ourselves
to the water below, like horseflies
charging at a pale blue glow.

Akinsdale Arena

Before the first cold white cuts mark the face
of the ice at Akinsdale, the rink attendant, stubble-jawed
forty-something in jeans and corduroy jacket,
uses the flat-top grill in the concession kitchen
where I work during my first year out of one school
and into another. He brings three brown eggs in half a carton,
a zip-lock of Montreal steak spice, a skinny cut of bright red beef
sealed beneath cellophane in its Styrofoam casket, so cheap
it has no marbling, no grey fat to keep it from drying out
on the grill. I do the day's prep, count cans of soft drinks,
Kit Kats and Twix bars and bags of chips, replace the previous
night's thick brown fryer oil with a new jug of Golden Canola
while the attendant cooks breakfast—only enough for himself.
He eats like he works: speechless and alone, with the stale gestures
of a person who knows what to expect of any given day.

All glazed over, eighteen and at work, I'll split stacks
of frozen patties, leave hot dogs to burst and shrivel
on the roller, pour water-thin hot chocolates
for hockey parents while the day's games play out—
novice to atom, bantam to midget, the junior Bs asking
a twoonie at the door. I was a left wing once, rubbed shoulders
with Plexiglas from end to dead end, watched teammates
pot hat tricks from the stained-wood bench. Now I'm fixed
on the pop and sizzle of that round cut on the grill, the tinny smell
of blood turned to steam. Even the permanent stench of sweat
and black rubber flooring laid to forgive steel-bladed steps
is not enough to make me forget the peppercorns, coriander,
dried garlic, coarse salt, hanging on with each quick flip.

During these morning-shift hours, when sleep clings
like static to the corners of my eyes and the cold follows
me in from the outside, I want another man's simple breakfast
more than the minimum wage I make or the youth
I've been charged with. More than the icy sheet of time
and potential that has been cleared for me. But only that. Never
his laps and laps with frigid hands on the Zamboni's vinyl wheel,
those last heavy shovelfuls of wet snow over the lip
of the gate, left to melt through the drain on the floor,
or each mandatory inspection of another surface restored.

The First Bus Back to the Suburbs

Cracks in the joint of the articulated bus
make it so I can't shake a cold so ubiquitous
in a year's time I will knot the thread of my life
to leave it. Passengers talk small through the fog
of their own breath. Beside me, an old woman
is looking for a doctor to call her own, says all the kids
nodding off on the university bus are studying
computers. What good will that do her when they're
young no longer and she *needs* them? A sudden stream
of January sun warms my face like aerosol
deodorant sprayed through the solitary flame
of a barbecue lighter. Jared and I used to burn
the signs on the wetland boardwalk that way,
scorch out the names of invasive wildflowers,
dull-feathered birds. Once we killed
a crow with a slingshot and a brick because
his dad paid us one purple bill each to do it.
Jared would grow up to break his hand on a boulevard
tree after he saw me with her at margarita madness,
haul me to the ground by my collar outside
a donair shop on Jasper Ave, spend every summer
since high school grading topsoil for one half
of Henday Drive and then the next.
It would be my fate to sleep my way
through grade twelve math, skin my knuckles
climbing the neighbour's roof while clutching
a souvenir bottle of mescal. But for now I freeze
on the first bus back to the suburbs. There are no stops
until I get off at home. On this short ride,
past the north side mattress depots and lumberyards,
everything is mercifully out of my hands.

Good Guilt

A disbeliever and a skeptic, I underestimated the house
red at a karaoke bar on Jasper Ave, spat my way back

to my parents' on the bench seat of Chris Rogers' sedan.
Half-dried saliva speckled my shoes and I left them

on while I draped myself around the toilet. When morning
interrupted, I found the ceramic cross that used to hang

in my room next to the door frame in pieces on the carpet.
It had been some time since the saviour and I had fallen out,

but I've always been a person of habit. That's why
the crucifix was still there on the wall for me

to smash it. The next time I feigned Catholic, I attended
the service after Chris fell from the balcony in Puerto Vallarta

and snapped his neck. Mostly now, I fear the demonic. Yesterday
I found so many grubs in a bag of pecans they appeared to flicker.

Six flies circled my desk, mark of the *Tabanus atratus*.
I cut the air with the fly swatter and incanted my good guilt:

 I didn't mean it. I didn't mean it.

White Cotton Socks

for Christopher Rogers

For the third night in a row I found you
in a dream I was having. You were
preparing to move from your childhood
home and I was helping you pack
your socks. I folded them, one into
the other, tossed them into a heap
on the bed. There was a pine dresser
drawer endlessly full of your
white cotton socks. Long ones
for playing ice hockey. Singles
with blown-out toes and grass stains.
Socks, woven thick, for working
at Grimshaw on the loading docks.
Your mother came and went
from the room, but never
acknowledged either of us.
She knew you were not
going anywhere, that you
were already gone. Something
we all knew in that world,
but are just beginning to know
in this one.

After the Neon Bowling Alley

I awoke to a light smothered
by the filth on my bedroom window
and a head split by its own cries
for cold water. In the driveway
was my father's grey quarter-
ton truck and in the bed of it,
a mock orange sapling
planted in a black plastic bucket.
You'll understand this filled me
with palpable dread as I half-recalled
how, after the neon bowling alley,
I'd pulled the price sign from
every planter in the Canadian Tire
parking lot, arranged them like
a pentagram star, then dragged
that shrub over the roots that gave
rise to cracks in the rounded
asphalt, to the ravine beyond,
across the slacking river, up hill
upon gradual hill, four clicks
at least, maybe more, to home.
Only to have it still be there
the next morning in full-budded
youth, throned above the concrete,
a mock orange mocking me.

Public Works

My father has always found his worth in work.
Each morning of that wasted summer, the first few
minutes of dry light shared at the kitchen counter
over instant black coffee and peanut butter toast.
He had his, I had mine. We did not say much.
After, I drove to the public works yard, stripped
down to briefs, climbed into bright orange
coveralls caked in mud, and joined the men
from Dig Crew to pilot half-ton trucks
packed with acetylene up and down the city's
reconstructed streets. I was some kind of sick
at nineteen, head going south to badlands,
rippling with pseudo-hallucinations of water bugs
in the sky. Pulled over when they became too much
for my kid mind, breathed into plastic bags,
blotted water from my bloodshot eyes. I told no one
about the trails of radio-colour each time I turned
my head, phosphorescent halos around every light.
Unfit, I taxied those tanks of fire around,
guided backhoes down past electrical lines
and gas pipes, torched rusted nuts and bolts
off hydrant stands twelve feet beneath my other
life. I dug graves in pristine ground, dangled
from a yellow tether down narrow sewer shafts
with a bucket and a beeper to detect the stinkdamp
gas they say will choke a young man quicker.
I poured chemicals in sewage grates to kill
the roots that clogged the line, wondering
what it might be like to be cleaned of life inside.
I kept at it for the money. But also as a duty
to the man who sat across from me each morning,

whose mechanical pride for me might leak a steady
song if I ever quit working. I had come to understand
the part of him that feared his son, the kind of man
I might become as I grew taller and thicker than him.

That uncertainty in raising a birch tree,
whose roots could be spreading anywhere,
taking hold of anything, underneath.

In American English

Aphids dry beneath the paint we lay at Devin's farmhouse in Arundel.
As boys, we slept in backyard tents, dreaming in American English.

Past the wheat pool is a trestle bridge. On either side, the water runs.
There are times the river holds so still, you could write it in American English.

Rows of poplars wait for spring. In this, they are my better.
Beside them, in her father's truck, we idle in American English.

The thinnest branches, thick with leaves, could not bear the early snowfall.
Like me, they bent and broke, then hung suspended in American English.

Here I call you each by name, and hope you'll take me back.
We are prairie roses, wild. Our parents named us in American English.

Another Thing Entirely

I don't need to talk about the ocean.
Who hasn't seen it stilled against some bay?
It pulls the clouds down so close
sometimes that I mistake myself
for drunk in their shallow haze.
Water will do that, play its tricks.
Though I've never seen the fog
as thick as that night we spent driving
through the Bow Valley flats.
Rawlick's knuckles, all ten of them
wrapped around the wheel, white and stiff.
Shaina with her head on his lap,
touching him like she always did.
He told me once that all of their arguments
would end with them pressed up
in the shower, or else on the stairs.
Now it's another thing entirely.
People sour on each other, and all that touching
can turn into an ocean, an expanse.

But I wouldn't have believed it then.
It was the three of us, together in one motion,
plunging on and on through one turn,
and then the next.

II

Bucky

after an interview with Bill McPherson

1.

well you know Kelly
born in Langenburg
Saskatchewan
to Bill and Linda
Buchberger
played his minor
in Langenburg
double-A midget
in Moose Jaw
for a year after
tier two with the
Melville Millionaires
Saskatchewan Junior

2.

that fire happened
he was twelve
got his leg burnt
that day
he never wore
socks again
I heard he wore
barefeet in his skates
all the time
what I believe
the story I heard
they went to the local
lake and wrapped
his legs
in mud

3.

next he played with
the Moose Jaw
Warriors
the Western
Hockey League
after the first year
Kelly was drafted
went to play with
the Oilers' farm
team in Nova Scotia
that's Halifax
for the '86–87 season
he was called up
played three
games of the playoffs
received his first
Stanley Cup ring
in Edmonton they won
the Stanley Cup

4.

he was a defensive
player yup
lots of penalties
oh yeah he was good
at fighting
not off hand

5.

and there's
another thing
all three players
on the line
from Moose Jaw
became the captains
of their teams
first time in history
one complete line
that was Kelly
for the Oilers
Fleury for the
Flames
and the guy
from Montreal
all became
captain the same
year but I forget
the guy's name
who played for
Montreal he played
for the Warriors too

6.

Kerri she played
volleyball played
for the University
of Regina
and she played
for Team Canada
'89–90–91
was a junior
national star then
on the national
team in '94
did the national
cup tour in '96
they won the right
to go to
the Olympics
in Georgia won
the Continental Cup
beating Puerto Rico
went to Atlanta
and did not win
huh that's all
also in Germany
and Spain
in the winter time
his other sister
is a City
of Edmonton
peace officer

7.

in '88 and '90
he received
his second and third
Stanley Cup rings
not yet
as captain
for Team Canada
'93 Munich Germany
Milan Italy they won
the gold medal
in Vienna Austria
they won the silver
he was traded
to Los Angeles
from the Kings
he was traded
to Pittsburgh
now what
year that was
I forget

8.

well he married
his high school girl
from high school
they had a boy
and a girl
still live in
Edmonton
they gotta be
in their twenties
now other than that
I don't know
nothing

9.

his job right now
he's manager
of the Oilers
player personnel
I don't know
what it is
exactly
I tried
to get a hold
of his mother
I can't
get a hold
of her to see
if she'll give
some more
information
but I can't get
a hold of her

10.

no I can't
tell you them
I don't know
none of them
I've got a picture
here of Kelly
holding the
Stanley Cup
if your mother
comes over
takes a picture
with her camera
she can send it
you have to tell her
if I get a hold
of his mother
I might get some
more but she's hard
to get a hold of
maybe she doesn't
want to talk
to me
I don't know

III

New to Me Still
and Probably Always

And it's true
I spent my whole life in fear of sharing my mind
but with a longing for it to be taken.

—Bianca Stone

I Am Not for This World Awake

Five blocks from this apartment, the tide
has served a final eviction notice to bull kelp

and capsized Dungeness left to suffocate in cool air
on a beach I never visit. When I was younger

and that much farther east, I used to pray
to sand dollars in a vase on my mother's vanity.

Now, while my thin sliver of the earth is still dragging
through its last moments of muddy darkness, I hope

for traffic sounds to drown out the calls
of small birds outside this single-pane window.

In Recognition of a Quarter-Century of Contribution to UMA

They gave him a bad watercolour: two men
surveying a dirt road flanked by standing
water and train tracks stretched thin to three
red grain elevators no longer in operation.
The men stand behind their yellow tripods,
measuring the distance between something
and nothing. It is almost winter. Everything
is dead or dying. The trees hold no leaves.
The canola, barbered down to stubble.

For twenty-five years my father has been
assessing, with the precision of a person
born into nothing, the unpaved road to
something. I have watched him mark
the milestones like the centimetre lines
on a ruler—kneeling at the edge of the teak
coffee table, raising the orange cat high
above his split-level empire of berber
carpet and second-hand furniture.

I Get a Phone Call from My Mother on a Wednesday Afternoon

A small something has been gnawing at
the corners of the patio table. Wood chips
collect around the parsley and sweet basil
seedlings beneath the barbecue—a gift
for my twenty-second birthday. The balcony
overlooks a stand of smooth-leaved elms
that tremble in any passing breeze,
and the Centre for the Deaf and Hard
of Hearing, where my once-partner sat in
an Al-Anon circle with me in mind.
The phone rings. My mother calls to say
a Christian prayer for two mounties,
shot dead twelve blocks from our family
home. No, she will not help me
with the rent. At the construction site,
the ignitions of sedans and pickups fire,
pistons push their tired cargo. Inside,
I close the blinds of crooked aluminum.
I'm still afraid of the world
and what I might do in it.

Apricot Ham

I've started to notice more,
he says to me. Yesterday:
how big the boulevard birch,
how thin the dog on its new diet
of oats and organic veal. Today
my father concerns himself
with the ham, bastes it
with a mixture of soya sauce
and apricot jam, slow
cooks it with indirect heat
and a pouch of applewood chips
for good measure.

He thought that all of this
would be over after a month,
but here we are partway through
September and the lawyer still hasn't
settled his severance. Can't work
another job until he gets his
two weeks for every year. Until
then, the barbecue will do.
The web video recipes starring
a man with no face in white
latex gloves will do. The coffee
dates to complain about the company
days will do. He forks the ham,
carves away a bit of the bark,
hands it, black and sweet, to me.
You could chew it for days
and never tire.

Black Friday, 1987, and Some Time After

The sky was a sack of dark green marbles,
each one clacking against the next, is what Mom
says about watching the storm sweep in
like gasoline spilled down Jasper Ave. She was
auditing a garment factory—a sweatshop, she says.
When the lights went dead: a hundred screaming
seamstresses, needles and thread stilled in the pitch
black basement. Driving home up Mark Messier Trail,
she counted ten ambulances. The tornado, three vortices
twisted together, had a mind of its own, tossed
the oil tanks and trailers of Refinery Row, forded
the rising North Saskatchewan, then tore a line
through the matchstick mobile homes of Evergreen.
For dessert, Mom says, *before it let the city be.*

I grew up a storm watcher, a weather channel connoisseur.
When prairie downbursts blew in, I counted seconds after
each lightning flash, before thunder. I knew where
was best to bank a mattress for cover, which room
to lock the dog in, which tables not to cower under.
To tell a scud from a funnel cloud, look for
rotation around a tight centre. I spotted it first,
sitting in a lawn chair on Lake Wabuman's shore,
no shelter, no cover for ten kilometres. We turned
ourselves to the water and watched the wall
of thunderheads topple toward us. A spiralling arm
reached down, raised the grey lake skyward. They came
together, and held. For how long, I don't remember.

How to Find Your Way in Strathcona County

No frost can stay on the steel or chrome,
warmed by the volumes of raw
and seething oil, the smell of which
is nondescript to those who find their way
by the pale blue light of the mercury vapour lamps,
glowing by the hundreds on Refinery Row.
Drive until you can count them
through the cylinders and smoke.
Go until you see the stacks, small fires
poised high into the night.
These are the stars that guide the north.

Ordinary

Take the Windsor chair, for instance,
four legs and a back to lean on,
arranged beneath the kitchen table,
a coat of rose-coloured paint
layered thinly above a sea foam
green and the original white.
For years, a seat for the dust that rests
in the rafters of my family's attic.
Given to my father by his Tante Lucille
(*Take* the damn thing! *Take* it!)
who tried to take my pépère
for what little he had left,
the cancer, too, about to take him
in his Sturgeon Hospital bed.

I was not alive to see this happen
and would never, myself, meet the man,
but my father tells me, *Take me home*,
made up most of what my pépère said.

Medicine Hat

In the bed next to Grandpa Bill's
the man called Pat is on the phone
with the cable company, cancelling his service.
He hangs up, peels a tangerine, talks about Medicine
Hat, where he worked during the war
testing mustard gas. A private at Suffield,
he carried out his orders—enter room, open canister,
breathe normally. He's lost so much
weight, he cannot stand. Grandpa Bill
is in a mood after the fever, cusses
out Grandma Julie as she wipes his forehead.
Pat tells him, *Just relax.*
Pat does not receive any guests,
has no cancer in his lungs, but something
just as bad, eats tangerines and drinks
Carnation instant breakfast
while settling his wife's estate.
The doctor enters, passes Pat, approaches
Grandpa's bed to offer him
a clean bill of health and his
professional opinion.
Take these. Drink water. Rest always.

Milk Separator

The faded chrome machine once split
skim milk and heavy cream on a farm
in Spy Hill that Grandpa ran away from
at seventeen. Cracked oak handle crank,
two spigots from a deep steel bowl,
all assembled over a heavy base
in the corner of his carless one-car garage.
Co-tenant to Auntie Lauralee's orange childhood
tricycle, wood planers and hand drills,
curling brooms, a *Saskatchewan bowling ball*—
that's what he calls it—pitted ball bearing
from the potash mine at Belle Plaine.

He lifts away Grandma's blue jersey bedsheets
from over a sun-bleached wooden Santa Claus,
asks if I would like to take it off his hands.
Parting is no great labour since he lost
his Julie, and each day turns over a little
easier than the last. Just yesterday he got out
of bed, tested the separator, dumped in a quart
of unpasteurized milk from the farmers' market,
worked the crank over and around until thick and thin
poured out the taps. It's antique, still works,
worth ten tanks of gas or one month's rent.
But he'll hold on to it. The shaft needs greasing
and it's heavier than any one person can lift.

Allowance

You plant lady's mantle
in your boulevard garden
as air turns to clear droplets
on the cold surfaces of things.
When night comes along,
someone comes along, too,
and pisses on your flowers.
Stomps their yellows and greens
into the wet dark of the dirt.
Pulls their shallow roots
up and out of the earth.
Takes even this small
allowance from you.

If fate is a vehicle,
we are tin cans in tow
losing our shape
on this pitted road.
Nothing is exempt from
being tied to the fender.
Even this. Even this.

The Best Way to Kill a Fish So Small

Snap its neck. I remember that
standing on a sheet of plywood
nailed to blue plastic barrels,
see-sawing on Kissinger Lake.
A cutthroat thrashes at the end
of my line, mouth begging
the air, dumb and noiseless.

On shore, an overalled man
presses his ear to a silent two-way
radio, drinks lemonade and rye
on the bench of a busted golf cart,
a rubber chicken impaled
on the exhaust pipe. Sells
nightcrawlers in soup cups,
says the best bait is live, picks
them himself from the lakeside
at night. Used to work
for the company that made
the exchange: Douglas fir
for swaths of grey on the slopes
of the Cowichan Valley.

I work my thumb past teeth,
into the smooth throat, bring
its head back until its body refuses
to follow, stiff, tearing at the gills.
Another trout jumps
for a taste of bright orange
synthetic bait suspended
like the points of Orion
on the black lake.

Carson Pegasus

Half a beer it maybe took him,
could be less or more,
to pull that first rainbow from the water,
Daniel saying nothing as he unhooked the fish,
crushed its skull with a collapse of his heel
and weaved the chain-link through its gill.
It was the first of many to float belly-up
off the seawall at Carson Pegasus
with Daniel's boot print pressed
into the scales and side.

And what a shame it was for me
to cast throughout the day and well
into the night—even the weeds feel like fish
when gone so long without a bite.
And what it was to be alone and drunk
and pacing in the absent light,
kicking cans of Coors
into the water, those who one time cared
for me, somewhere, caring for another.
And I for no one or nothing.

Hidden within the brush and high cattail grass
were the bodies of trout, the youngest trout,
with their pretty scales and paltry meat.
Some catch so many they choose
to keep only their proudest.
The others rotted in the August sun,
to rise in air, an offering.
Come morning we learned their scent,
remembering something, shapeless and distant.
Speechless from the smell of it.

Night Residue

I dream I'm in love with the quieter
of two twins and waking hurts
so I force myself back
to sleep where for a while
I don't dream but at some point
my mind becomes the sun on one half
of a hill of trilobites and dinosaur dust
at the foot of an ocean
that has since sunk
with the shyness of a child
further into its lonely place
on the earth and the water
is so clear I can see
pretty orange fish flash by
in schools like smoke above
the last coals of a fire
and seashells like shingles of marble
on the roof of a structure collapsed
under the terrible weight
of beauty and not a person
anywhere, not even me.

Cribbage

It has been one year and four months since I slid
a kitchen chair around the living room and picked

assorted nails from their coops in the drywall. In the same
time it takes a newborn to stretch its vocal cords and mew

along with a parent's cradle song, I have learned to embrace
the light of the sun at its most unwanted hour, to pick

tangles of her black hair from the corners of the baseboards
and turn one knotted shoulder to the past. She enters

the room in a canary yellow tutu, red pirate hat
angled on her head, and does a shaky pirouette.

I was six points back of the skunk line last night
when she pegged out and our audition ended, a success.

Crokinole

I have waited in thirty-below,
an hour in an uncertain queue,
to be readmitted into a former life.
That smell—burnt oil, ice salted
into water, seldom cleaned taps
of the Strat Hotel. A safe amount
is always half. Men with prairie stock
and too much disposable cash, shit-faced
on their five off from the oil patch,
break each other over the hoods
of parked cars for a chance
to get the blood running
to their hands again.
The used car dealership across
Whyte Ave is the blue of the crescent
moon nightlight in my childhood
bedroom. I could've stayed, chest
fastened with cold snaps, chronic nosebleeds
each December. But when you cleared
the discs on your last turn,
I had a clear line to your centre.

Exact Fare

A young woman is missing
the extra dollar twenty-five
it takes to ride the Tsawwassen
Ferry Terminal Express.
The driver decides to allow it.
She takes a seat and tries
to wipe the drops of water
from the window, but
they're on the other side.

Exit

Did brown bats beam
like dark matter from pine
to lodgepole pine
when Brandon left you
in the tent, dead-centre
of the night, to consider
the virtue of your sexuality?

Had I been there with you
in the park beside the power
plant, camping on the gravel
shores of Lake Wabamun,
we could have seen him
off towards his failed
photography hobby and had
our first honest talk.

But you're as hard
and sharp as anyone. I trust
you slept alright.

Pembina River, August '09

There was something
familiar in the way
Dan was tuning his guitar,
the notes skipping
across the river
like water bugs in play
to the distant bank
and back again.

Certain noises rest within
the hollows of my body
and remind me
it's been a while
since I've heard anything
for the first time.

On Being Threatened over Red Willow Park

St. Albert, Alberta

The black patina of wood tar
stinks and sticks to the soles of our shoes
as Matthew and I follow the rails
over a darkness named Sturgeon,
no longer a river but the last slow leak
of what inspired French Christians
to raise a white chapel and a convent
and this trestle bridge at the bottom
of a valley—a dry scar against the grain
of the boreal plains. It's Canada Day.
I've come home to see my grandmother
through to the afterlife. The only light:
red and white Catherine wheels
scorching the sky over Seven Hills.
Those distant cracks colour the boredom
of adolescent boys and girls leaning
into each other and another long July.

Matthew and I are alone on the bridge,
suspended in a bit of quiet, until two
men emerge from the treeline.
Their steps sink into gravel, words
slur and swell in volume. We back
onto the platform, four rotting planks
and a rust-gnawed railing, and they pass
then turn to say that if the two of us
were thrown down into the riverbed,
had our necks cut from right to left,
or our heads caved in around

the flat-bottom steel tracks, no one
would know who to point a finger at.
They laugh and walk away and I feel
the whole small world of this place
ripple through my hair and in my legs
as if a freight train from Redwater
or Westlock were ploughing on past me.
To think that all of it could end like this:
the brunt of some bad joke told
by two cheap drunks on a bridge meant
for trains in a town raised by saints
under the scarce light of fireworks.

Christmas Morning, Boundary Bay

For now the Pacific, new to me still
and probably always, is as flat
and impassive as the kettle lakes
back home—prairie potholes dug
a manageable distance from one bank
to the other by a glacial advance
and retreat, several lifetimes before
anything like a home existed,
when the years were longer
and the winter was permanent.

At home, where the winter is nearly
permanent, my father was born between
those bodies of water and never left.
My mother moved there after him,
an army brat. Then her father retired from
the Goose Squadron to drive the night
bus down Whyte Ave. Her mother, grounded
when her driver's licence expired, managed
the glassy lengths of the Hudson's Bay
cosmetics counter until she expired herself.

In Boundary Bay, we are outnumbered
by the gulls and the sky is opening
after days of rain. My mother calls, tells me
Grandma is still humming in the power lines
above her plain military wife's grave, that Grandpa
hasn't stopped chewing cigars and blowing
snow from the sidewalk to the boulevard
strip, until it returns, from above
or elsewhere, like an ache that goes
and comes, to the concrete again.

Notes

The epigraph of section one is from Philip Levine's poem "Lame Ducks, McKesson and Robbins, 1945" from *The Simple Truth* (1993).

"Sociables" is inspired by the song "I Saw a Ghost Last Night" written by Troy Snaterse and Altameda. The poem is dedicated to Mitch Tanner.

"Categorical Imperative" is inspired by Immanuel Kant's concept of the categorical imperative.

"The First Bus Back to the Suburbs" is for Jared Snidal.

"Imperatives," "Good Guilt" and "White Cotton Socks" are for Christopher Rogers.

"Carson Pegasus" is for Dan Rawlick.

"Cribbage" and "Crokinole" are for Mallory Tater.

"On Being Threatened over Red Willow Park" is for Matthew Punyi.

"Bucky" is an erasure of the transcript from an interview I conducted with my grandfather, Bill McPherson, in December of 2016.

The epigraph in section three is from the titular poem of Bianca Stone's collection *Someone Else's Wedding Vows* (2014).

Earlier versions of these poems have appeared in *Poetry is Dead, Sport Literate, Existere, The Maynard, Glass Buffalo, The Literary Review of Canada, Cede, Arc, The City Series: Edmonton* (Frog Hollow Press), *Alberta Views, NewPoetry.ca, EVENT, Prairie Fire, The Walrus* (online), *30 Under 30* (In/

Words Press), *Big Smoke, Eighteen Bridges, The Malahat Review, Sustenance* (Anvil Press), CV2, *The Rusty Toque* and a chapbook, *Good for Nothing* (Anstruther Press, 2017). Thank you to the editors of each.

Acknowledgements

Thank you to my parents, Ann and Marcel, and brother and sister, Marc and Gabrielle, for their constant love and support. To friends and family back home in St. Albert, Alberta, thank you for all the inspiration.

Thank you to Nightwood Editions for making this book real, especially Silas White, Carleton Wilson and Amber McMillan. Thanks to Erik Grice for the beautiful cover art.

Thank you to my teachers for their generous guidance while writing these poems, especially Rhea Tregebov, Karen Solie, Rachel Rose, Ian Williams and Ken Babstock.

Thank you to Kayla Czaga, Raoul Fernandes and Eduardo C. Corral for their words and encouragement.

Thank you to my peers at the University of British Columbia and to the poets who fill our home with warmth every second Tuesday for workshop. I'm especially thankful to Shaun Robinson, Selina Boan, Chris Evans, Dominique Bernier-Cormier and Adèle Barclay. There is so much strength and compassion in our community and you're all too many to name.

Finally, this book would not have been possible without the lessons, love and support from my partner, Mallory Tater. Thank you, for everything—because it has been everything.

About the Author

Curtis LeBlanc was shortlisted for the *Walrus* Poetry Prize in 2016, received the Readers' Choice Award in *Arc*'s Poem of the Year Contest and was shortlisted for *CV2*'s Young Buck Poetry Prize. His writing has appeared in *The Malahat Review*, *Eighteen Bridges*, *The Literary Review of Canada*, *Prairie Fire*, *EVENT*, *Geist*, *Arc*, *CV2*, *The Rusty Toque* and others. He is managing editor of Rahila's Ghost Press, co-host of Tonic Reading Series, web editor at Nineteen Questions and an occasional hockey columnist for NHL Numbers. He served as executive editor of promotions at *PRISM international* in 2016–17. His poetry chapbook *Good for Nothing* was published by Anstruther Press in 2017. LeBlanc was born and raised in St. Albert, Alberta, and lives in Vancouver, BC.

PHOTO CREDIT: Allie Kenny